Edmund S. Foster

On medical provision for railroads as a humanitarian measure,

As well as a source of economy, to the companies: in two papers, read

respectively before the N.Y. State Medical Society, Feb. 5, 1862 and the

Surgical Section of the New York Academy of

Edmund S. Foster

On medical provision for railroads as a humanitarian measure,
As well as a source of economy, to the companies: in two papers, read respectively before the N.Y. State Medical Society, Feb. 5, 1862 and the Surgical Section of the New York Academy of

ISBN/EAN: 9783337731700

Printed in Europe, USA, Canada, Australia, Japan

Cover: Foto ©ninafisch / pixelio.de

More available books at **www.hansebooks.com**

ON

𝔐𝔢𝔡𝔦𝔠𝔞𝔩 𝔓𝔯𝔬𝔳𝔦𝔰𝔦𝔬𝔫 𝔣𝔬𝔯 𝔕𝔞𝔦𝔩𝔯𝔬𝔞𝔡𝔰,

AS A

HUMANITARIAN MEASURE,

AS WELL AS

A SOURCE OF ECONOMY TO THE COMPANIES.

𝔍𝔫 𝔗𝔴𝔬 𝔓𝔞𝔭𝔢𝔯𝔰.

READ RESPECTIVELY BEFORE THE

N. Y. State Medical Society, Feb. 5, 1862,

AND THE

Surgical Section of the New York Academy of Medicine, Oct. 28th, 1862.

BY

EDMUND S. F. ARNOLD, M.D.,

JEFFERSON COLLEGE, PHILADELPHIA, MEMBER OF THE ROYAL COLLEGE OF SURGEONS OF
ENGLAND, RESIDENT FELLOW OF THE NEW YORK ACADEMY OF
MEDICINE, OF YONKERS, N. Y.

NEW YORK:
BAILLIÈRE BROTHERS, 440 BROADWAY.
1862.

CONTENTS.

PREFACE.

Some two months since the author was called to see a poor fellow, whose leg was said to have been broken by a fall from the cars. He had been asleep, passed his destination, and, on going out half awake, was probably bewildered, and fell off the platform. He was found lying on a straw mattress, in an empty building used as a temporary barrack, on a bedstead improvised by means of an old door on a couple of barrels, and a blanket thrown over him. On examining the injured limb, the ankle-joint and bones for some inches above it proved to be fearfully crushed and exposed through a gaping lacerated wound seven or eight inches long. Expecting a simple case of fracture, some splints had been taken to the spot. No one would take such a case in, there were no facilities at hand, and the best that could be done for him, as happens in numerous similar cases, was to put up the limb as well as circumstances permitted, let him await the next train, and then forward him in the baggage car to one of the city hospitals, fifteen or sixteen miles distant.

To provide for all such unfortunate victims of railway casualty a temporary refuge, where the first duties of humanity may be performed, and where they can be taken care of until such time as they can be removed with safety, is the object advocated in the following pages. To the arguments employed to prove

the necessity of local medical provision for railroads, and to the
simplicity of the plans proposed for its accomplishment, as well
as to their inexpensiveness, considering the magnitude and life-
saving results of the object to be attained, the attention of the
Legislature and of the travelling public, which, after all, com-
prises nearly the whole community, is respectfully and earnestly
solicited.

Had the author been aware, when writing the first paper,
that a legislative measure bearing upon the subject was in pre-
paration, its style would have been somewhat different; but as
after all the plans for medical provision remain the same, he
prefers to place it before the public in the form in which it
received the approval and endorsement of the representatives
of the general professional body of the State.

To carry out efficiently the plans proposed, or others with a
similar object, mutual concessions must be made by the railroad companies and the public. In the admirable measure of
which some account is given in the second paper, the latter
receive a full *quid pro quo* for all that is asked of them.

The testimonials and endorsements at the end are necessarily
not numerous, as the different pamphlets heretofore published
have had only a private, and of course limited circulation.
Such as they are, however, they could not well be stronger,
comprising, as they do, the approval of two of the largest medical bodies of the State, namely, the New York State Medical
Society and the Surgical Section of the New York Academy
of Medicine. To those may be added the Westchester County
Medical Society, and the names of nearly every Professor of
Surgery in the Medical Colleges of New York City. The number of societies and of individual names might be largely in-
creased, no doubt, if the professional duties of the author had
allowed him time to make application.

To the professional body at large he has felt himself deeply indebted for the cordial sympathy and generous encouragement they have throughout afforded him in the prosecution of his task so far.

YONKERS, *November*, 1862.

ON

MEDICAL PROVISION FOR RAILROADS

AS A HUMANITARIAN MEASURE, AS WELL AS A SOURCE
OF ECONOMY TO THE COMPANIES.

Read before the New York Medical Society, February 5, 1862.

By EDMD. S. F. ARNOLD, M.D., M.R.C.S.E.,

DELEGATE FROM WESTCHESTER COUNTY.

WE live in an age when calls upon the public in aid of suffering humanity are seldom disregarded. A need may not be
immediately recognised, but, once perceived, there are always
found in the community actively benevolent minds, who with
heart and purse betake themselves to the task, and resolutely
and energetically keep the public mind alive until the desired
object is attained. In how many noble institutions have these
efforts culminated, institutions for the aged and infirm, for deaf-
mutes, for the blind and the lame, reformatory establishments
of various kinds, as well as noble hospitals both for general and
special purposes. Then, again, our coasts are well supplied
with life-boats, or mortars to send a rope to the rescue of a
perishing crew; well organized fire companies are ever on the
alert to guard our lives and property from the ravages of fire—
would that I could add they were well supplied with fire
escapes, for the benefit of our over-crowded tenement houses,
too often limited for egress to a single narrow staircase—and
hundreds, I might say thousands, have been saved from a watery
death by the active exertions and widely circulated regulations
of the Humane and similar societies. With institutions so
numerous and so varied, one might readily believe that provision was already made, in one way or other, for every class of
victims to sudden casualty; yet, with all this, there is still a
great and pressing want to be supplied, an evil of gigantic pro-
portions yet to be grappled with, one not only of a deeply
interesting character to our profession, but of such vital importance to the travelling public, that we may well wonder it has
never yet attracted attention.

Within the last half century our mode of land transit has
been entirely revolutionized. The old stage coach has gradu-

2

ally given way to the railway engine with its thundering train of cars. A vast network of railroads spreads itself out over the land, bringing the most distant points within easy reach of each other, and by the cheapness, speed, and, in the main, safety of the mode of travel, inducing tens of thousands, who probably under the old system would never have found themselves at any period of their lives ten miles away from the house in which they were born, to now traverse the continent without a thought of inconvenience or danger.

Let, however, the iron horse, usually so tractable to human guidance, be but for a moment interfered with in its course, and it becomes a crushing, tearing monster, breaking and splintering cars, scattering their mutilated occupants around in all directions, and giving to the ground the appearance of a recent battle-field. It is useless to say that all this is unnecessary and may be avoided. Apart from accidents arising from carelessness of employees, or neglect of regulations or signals, or switches, leading to collisions, to driving trains through open drawbridges into the river beneath, or to running cars off the road and over precipices by too great a rate of speed on heavy curves, there are numerous unlooked-for causes of disaster, among which may be enumerated, the straying of cattle on the track, the loosening of a rail, breaking of an axle, springing of a wheel from frost or defective casting, the gradual undermining of an embankment by water, the falling of a piece of rock on the track just previous to the arrival of a train, and many other causes, that will occur to our minds on reflection; so that while all that human forethought, care, and well devised regulations can do has been tried, we nevertheless are every now and then startled by the ominous heading in our newspapers of "Fearful Catastrophe" on this or that railroad, followed by harrowing details, and terminating in a long list of killed and injured. Nor is it only by these great accidents that life and limb are jeopardized; still more numerous are the cases of individual injury to passengers, employees, or others, arising, it is true, from want of care or thoughtlessness on their own part, yet none the less deserving of sympathy and of our best efforts in their behalf.

Public attention having never yet been fairly directed to this matter few are aware of the magnitude of the question under consideration. By the kindness of a friend I have been supplied with a copy of the Report of the State Engineer for the year ending September 30, 1860, from which I may here be allowed to make one or two extracts. A comparative statement for the years 1856 to 1860, inclusive, a period of five years, of railroad accidents on thirty lines of this state, furnishes the following facts:

11

PASSENGERS.		EMPLOYEES.		OTHERS.	
Killed.	Injured.	Killed.	Injured.	Killed.	Injured.
1856	18	78	48	18	107	27
1857	11	36	47	26	65	33
1858	20	142	29	25	67	46
1859	10	33	28	24	81	48
1860	13	36	28	17	111	45

Making a total of six hundred and eighty-three killed and six hundred and twenty-four injured, or thirteen hundred and seven in all, an average of two hundred and sixty-one per annum. Many of the above railroads are short lines, and easily supervised and kept in order, so that serious accidents are comparatively few in number, while five of them are mere city roads, the cars being drawn by horse power. I will therefore take five of the leading roads, with a total length of thirteen hundred and thirty-eight miles, and give the numbers killed and injured thereon in the above five years :

PASSENGERS.		EMPLOYEES.		OTHERS.	
Killed.	Injured.	Killed.	Injured.	Killed.	Injured.
47	223	139	68	342	121

Making a total of five hundred and twenty-eight killed and four hundred and twelve injured, or nine hundred and forty in all, an average of one hundred and eighty-eight per annum. Most of the above railroads lie mostly within the state, and there are on the whole few, if any, to be found better managed, while many in other parts will certainly ill compare with them either in construction or management. To consider this question in all its magnitude we should extend our inquiry to lines in other parts of the Union and to other countries, but for all present purposes to deal with our own state is sufficient.

What an awful sacrifice of life, in part at least unnecessary, what a fearful amount of human suffering the above figures cover! When we speak of so many killed, it is not thereby meant instantly killed; fortunate, indeed, are they in comparison with those allowed to sink and die in a few hours from the total absence of everything requisite to meet their condition, or

12

to give them a chance of life. We know, to a certainty, that
every now and then a terrible accident will occur, though we
cannot fix either the time or the locality ; we know also, that,
where it does occur, there is not a rag on hand to staunch a
bleeding wound, there is not a single appliance within reach of
any medical man, who might happen to be in the cars, to enable
him to render effective service, and this leads naturally to a very
important part of my subject, namely, that of immediate management of the injured, under the present system, or rather
under the want of it.

I think it will be conceded that, taken as a whole, railway
casualties may be regarded as about the most fatal that surgeons
meet with, and as they occur often in out of the way places,
much valuable time, even under the most favorable circumstances, is lost before they can be put under efficient permanent
treatment. Leaving out of the question those instantly killed,
among the injured who die within a short period, many will be
found whose injuries would not be likely to prove fatal under
other circumstances, but in whom intense excitement, in addition to the injury, is followed by rapid and fatal prostration. In
others again, whose injuries are more severe, and perhaps
accompanied by much loss of blood, the collapse is proportion-
ally severe from the commencement, and they sink before
assistance can be obtained, or when they get it are so far
reduced that the case has become hopeless. In the former
class patients should be at once removed from the scene of
excitement, and prompt measures taken to allay nervous irrita-
tion, as well as to encourage them by letting them feel and see
that they will be almost immediately well and efficiently provided for; in the latter hæmorrhage, if present, should be
arrested, means taken to promote reaction, and the sufferers
placed in the least painful position, until a station is reached,
where they can be attended to. Are these things done? I
think the answer generally must be, no. Could they be done?
I say, emphatically, to a great extent, yes. How, will be considered in another part of this article.

Among the recorded causes of individual injury are such as
the following : Brakeman fell from train—leg cut off; engineer
fell from engine—killed; passenger fell from platform while
stepping from one car to another—limbs crushed; arm torn
off by coming in contact with pier of a bridge while carelessly
thrusting the member out of a window. Again, we read of
persons with legs and arms crushed or cut off while crossing or
walking along the track, and dying a day or two after. Now,
let us suppose from some one or other of these causes, a leg is
crushed in a locality far away from any town. The train is

stopped, and the sufferer is quickly surrounded by a curious and sympathizing crowd. Pocket-handkerchiefs are freely offered for bandages; and if he is a poor man he is deposited on the floor of the baggage car; if a passenger, on seats in the best way circumstances permit; sometimes, however, on the bare floor too. And so they go on; every jar or unsteady movement of the cars causing intense pain to the victim, until a station is reached, where he is deposited and left to ————, Providence or chance, as we like to term it. The train pursues its way, and the temporary excitement is quickly forgotten. But let us return to the injured man, and see the case to the end. The nearest doctor is sent for, who, perhaps, when he arrives, does not know what to do, and promptly concludes that the patient will die; nothing can be done for him. Unwilling so to relinquish life, the sufferer sends for another, perhaps from a long distance, who, on reaching the spot, proceeds to do all that is necessary; but too much time has been lost, and the result is chronicled in a couple of lines in some local paper, which attracts little attention, and finally he figures as one killed in the annual railway report. Let a great accident occur, by which a train is wrecked in a similar locality, and what a terrible scene of confusion presents itself. Doctors are sent for in all directions, good, bad, and indifferent; and ere now, a whole hospital staff has been telegraphed to proceed to the scene of disaster. They cannot leave their duties, and assistants are sent, of course. Every one goes to work upon his own responsibility; the want of previous provision, of system and proper management are painfully felt, and loss of life and limb, and heavy pecuniary damages to the company, are the result. I do not mean to say that matters are always as bad as here represented; but I do assert, that when they are not, it is owing to accidental favoring circumstances rather than to proper provision; and that our present arrangements are not such as the claims of humanity imperatively demand at our hands.

As cases of personal experience must be necessarily limited, I must request to be allowed to quote one or two, already published in a small pamphlet written by me, rather with a view to break ground on this important question than as a full exposition of it. On the 18th of January, 1860, a way train ran into an express train, stationary on the line; the cause recorded, being want of attention to signals, killing four, and injuring six persons. Among the former was a lady, who died in our village the same evening. Having in the former article alluded to, quoted this case somewhat incorrectly, I will now give the testimony of a very competent physician on the inquest, copied from one of our local papers, which I have been fortunate enough to obtain. He says: "I was with Mrs. F——— from the time she was taken out of the wreck until she died; there was a compound fracture of both bones of the left leg, and a lacerated wound on the upper and internal part of the thigh; there were also bruises about the head, and on the left arm, but not, as I considered, dangerous; I suppose the cause of her death to have been primarily the nervous shock to her system with its consequent depression; and, secondarily, loss of blood; there was no evidence of internal injury sufficient to cause death; little was done for her beyond administering stimulants; all was done that I deemed proper, except that she should have been placed in a position to have received more speedy attention; I advised her being left at Tarrytown, the first stopping-place, but it was thought best, by those who had her in charge, that she should proceed to New York so as to be among her friends. She was finally taken off at Yonkers, and died about 7 o'clock in the evening. Here we have the whole matter. Everything was done that was deemed proper by a talented practitioner, *except* that she should have been placed in a position to receive more speedy attention. Here is the origin of a vast amount of mortality; here is the very thing that first suggested to my mind years ago the necessity for some special provision. In this case, the shock to the system was very severe, but could hardly have been greater than in the one I shall presently contrast with it; and the actual injuries were far less in amount.

Now, had the sufferer been gently removed to the nearest town or flag station, and her necessities promptly attended to, instead of time being lost, in carrying her on from place to place, a downward impetus being thereby given to already depressed and rapidly failing vital powers, might not the result have been different, and not only a valued life saved, but liability on the part of the company to the highest amount of individual damages avoided?

By way of contrast let us take the following case: In October, 1857, a boy, eleven years of age, jumped out of the baggage car of an express train, at full speed against the rocks, in a cutting, and, rebounding on the track, was picked up, horribly mangled. His injuries were as follows: The left foot and leg, from midway below the knee, completely smashed and in part torn away, fracture of the right thigh, compound fracture of the right leg midway below knee, both bones protruding, compound fracture of the right great toe, and a severe scalp wound of about three inches in length. When we add the fearful violence to the general system necessary to cause such a mass of injuries the case might well seem hopeless. He was quickly removed to his parents' residence, and medical assistance promptly at hand. I had the satisfaction of discharging him sound, of course with exception of loss of one leg below knee, after four months' attendance. There cannot be a doubt that had this boy been carried, in the usual way, twenty miles, to a distant hospital, he would have been added to the list of railway victims, and his death regarded as a matter of course, instead of growing into a fine, intelligent lad, and, supplied with a Palmer's patent leg, being actually employed, not long since, as runner, by the New York agent of that valuable apparatus. In this case everything favored prompt attendance. The train was little more than a mile from the station, and at the moment of the accident another was coming up in the opposite direction which brought him back ; carriages were in waiting for this due train, in one of which he was immediately removed home ; another surgeon and myself were on the spot almost as soon as he arrived there, and, desperate as the case appeared to be, the saving of time proved to be the means of saving life.

In February, 1854, messengers came to the village, between 3 and 4 A.M, stating that the bridge at the creek had broken through, that a car-load of passengers was submerged, and medical assistance needed. It was a bitter cold dark morning. I hastily gathered all that I thought might be useful, and, after several times narrowly escaping a capsize in snow-banks, reached the spot. Matters were not so bad as had been represented. One engine had got safely across ; the second, for there were two, had gone down with the express baggage car, in deep water, and the passenger car rested on the top of the latter, hanging half-way over the end of a broken track, thus allowing the few passengers to escape. Two scalded firemen had already been attended to. I made inquiries whether any others were hurt, but could learn nothing satisfactory, the employees seeming to regard me rather as an interloper than in any other light; I consequently started for the scene of the accident on the New York side. It was still dark, and on reaching the drawbridge, where the rail was laid along single timbers, which afforded the only means of crossing, these were so covered with ice that, after a few steps, I found it impossible to get over without the greatest risk of being blown off on to masses of ice below, so I turned and went home. I subsequently learned that I had been within a hundred feet of the express messenger, who would not leave his charge, and was suffering intensely from a sprained ankle, and for whose relief I might have done much, while assistance did not arrive from the city for several hours afterwards. Lucky was it for him that his injuries were no worse.

One more case and I have done with this part of my subject.

Some two years since a man threw himself down under an empty passenger car on the off track and went to sleep. Meantime the train came along, backed up and took off the empty car, which went over both the legs of the sleeper, who had not been observed. Here was a case at a station. I shortly after arrived and found him lying on the floor of one of the waiting rooms in the midst of a large crowd, with both legs fearfully crushed and bleeding profusely. What was to be done now was the question. Nobody would take him in, for he was but a poor loafer, and certainly nothing could be done where he was; the only alternative therefore was to staunch the bleeding, and as a train was soon coming up, he was bundled up in the best way circumstances permitted, and so sent as usual in the baggage car to the City Hospital with a result easily foreseen. His chances of life were perhaps but small, but even that little was denied him, and he died almost as soon as he arrived.

These cases, which might be multiplied *ad infinitum*, those occurring in one place being only repetitions of what takes place in another, go far to prove that none of our present institutions are sufficient to meet the peculiar wants of the injuries under consideration; that as many sink from shock and from the length of time that elapses before they are subjected to treatment, half an hour or an hour often determining the question of life or death, it becomes the imperative duty of the railroad companies, as well as their interest from the great pecuniary losses they are subjected to, to make some special provision adapted at least to relieve the immediate pressing necessities of those who may be injured on their lines, and thus place them in a condition for future successful treatment.

Having arrived thus far, I think it is made sufficiently apparent that the present state of things involves injustice to the public as travellers, who are all equally liable to injury; injustice to the public again as stockholders, by the amounts wasted in litigation or damages for real or spurious injuries, and in this the widow and orphan, whose little means are invested, are as much interested as the merchant and capitalist; injustice to the injured, who cry in vain for help when it is most needed; and, finally, injustice to our profession, whose members have too often to give their time, labor, and skill, gratuitously, and I may here observe, that in all cases of this class I have had to do with, I have but in one received any remuneration. *We* may not ignore the claims of humanity, nor do we wish to; but to that public, on whom after all the great burden of the wrong falls. I say: do also your part in satisfying those claims, strengthen our hands, give us needful appliances and conveniences, thus enabling us to use whatever skill we may possess to the best effect, and while we shall still gain little pecuniarily, you will be gainers in every way, you will mainly reap all the benefits.

Assuming the necessity for medical provision for railroads as established, I shall now proceed to develop practical plans for the accomplishment of this object. It is clear that the appointment of a surgeon, or a corps of them, at the main termini would not avail, nor would it answer to appoint paid surgeons on the line, who might never be employed. It must be borne steadily in mind, that our object is not to make permanent provision for the injured, though it may be used as such when desired, but merely to bridge over that fearful and fatal gap which intervenes between the time of the infliction of the injury, and that when the sufferer can be handed over to the surgeon of his own choice; thereby affording to the latter as good a chance of curing his patient as though he had taken possession of him from the first moment. To meet on the one hand the requirements of the case without infringing on the just rights of companies on the other, the provision must be *sui generis*. An accident may be recorded in one locality this week, the next may occur a hundred miles away, yet the same provision should extend equally to both without subjecting the respective companies to unnecessary expense. Such is the problem to be solved. I propose to consider the question under two heads: first, by arrangements along the line; secondly, by arrangements in the cars, by one or other of which, or by combinations of both, we can effectually secure the desired end on every railroad in existence.

First, then, as to arrangements along the line: and here I shall again avail myself of what I have previously written. Let each company appoint at its main terminus a medical inspector, with the rank of assistant superintendent. The duties of this officer would be to organize the line into districts; to issue medical regulations, with sanction of the general superintendent, to whom he would be subordinate; to receive and to collate reports; and to act as medical adviser of the Board of Directors in all pecuniary and other transactions with their district surgeons, to be presently mentioned. His duties would be of a confidential character, and he should be entirely in the interests of the company. His functions being multifarious, he should be a salaried officer; but as his duties would not interfere very materially with the requirements of private practice, his salary need not be a large one. Now, where an accident occurs, every railway servant is willing to assist, and does the best he can—often, however, acting very injudiciously for want of knowing better: one of the first duties, therefore, of the inspector, after organizing his department, should be to issue a simple code of directions to station-masters and flagmen, instructing them what to do previous to the arrival of a medical man in cases of accident. For instance, if a person is bleeding from a wound, the employees should be directed and shown how to apply a pad and bandage; and so a man may be saved from bleeding to death. If the sufferer is pale and chilly, with cold extremities, the railway official should be instructed to make a bed on his stretcher, to heat a brick and put it to the feet, also to administer a little warm tea at intervals, thereby often saving a man from sinking to death; and when a medical man arrives, instead of having to abandon the patient as a hopeless case, reaction may be commencing, affording encouragement to bestow his most strenuous efforts, or the powers of life may be so far restored that he can decide and act upon the necessary treatment at once. So much for the duties of the inspector.

In the next place, let the companies appoint district surgeons, unsalaried, but payable for actual services rendered, at the principal towns along the line, and not exceeding from ten to fifteen miles apart—the district of each to extend to the flag station nearest to midway between any two. The principal advantage attending such regular appointments would be that, where medical assistance was not immediately at hand, the employees would know exactly where to send for a competent practitioner. At each such surgical station, a small room should be set apart on the ground floor, furnished with an iron cot bedstead and bedding, a stretcher with mattress and pillow, a small table, one or two common chairs, and a small wood-stove, by which, if required, the room could be heated in a few minutes in winter, or hot water or a brick for application to the feet any time. I may here observe, that if the companies did their part, I have no doubt each surgeon could raise among his own friends and patients not only enough to furnish the main station, but also to provide every flag station, with a stretcher and mattress to be kept always ready for use. The surgeon might also keep at the station a little linen, lint, bandages, sponges, a few splints, and such minor articles for immediate use. He should also make it a rule to carry a tourniquet. In case of an accident, a stretcher and bed could be obtained from the nearest flag station, or those from the adjoining ones if several were seriously hurt, and the medical officer summoned, also those of adjoining stations, if necessary, as well as any competent medical men in the vicinity. If any injury were too severe to risk removal, the patient could be carried to the nearest flag station until the immediate danger had subsided; where practicable, however, he should be carried to the district station, his immediate wants there attended to, and provision made for safe removal. When a surgeon is summoned to the scene of an accident, he should have the right to avail himself of any passing train, that as little time as possible might be lost; and it should be his duty to examine carefully into the amount of injuries sustained, and to keep notes of the same for future refreshment of his memory; also to furnish a copy to the inspector, to be kept on file at the chief office. In cases of fraudulent or exaggerated claims upon companies, their medical officers would become most important witnesses; and I believe the amount thus saved would far exceed all costs, and tend greatly to diminish litigation.

By such arrangements if a person were injured severely on the line, passenger or otherwise, he would be laid on a comfortable mattress, his limbs arranged in the position affording most comfort, and so be carried by hand on a stretcher into or out of the cars without further disturbance until he reaches his destination. If several were injured, messengers might be sent to the adjoining flag stations, or the engine and tender detached thither; and so, in a short time, beds would be brought to the spot, and our first great need supplied. If any medical men were at hand, they could at once render valuable assistance; meanwhile, the district surgeon would be sent for, who, on his arrival, would take authoritative charge, and promptly and efficiently proceed to do whatever could be accomplished by a surgeon of skill and judgment. System and order would work out their natural results, suffering would be diminished, and life oftener saved. With the general introduction of such a system, we should have heard the last of a railway victim, with reaction approaching and returning circulation, awakening, perhaps, after a twenty miles' ride, to intense suffering, with the hard floor of a baggage car for his bed, a coat rolled up for his pillow; then having to endure the almost insufferable agony of removal, with broken limbs dangling or awkwardly handled, to a carriage; and from thence once more, with powers now for the second time prostrated, to the bed, from whence he is never destined to rise again.

The above plan would be very well suited to such a road as the Hudson River Railroad, where there are flag stations at almost every mile, and where important towns are near together. Many of the lines, however, run through thinly populated districts, with long distances intervening between stations and flag stations. Here, our apparatus would not be sufficiently accessible; and we need, therefore, some slightly different provision. This must be furnished by appliances in the cars themselves. In many of these, there is at the end a small portion partitioned off, and containing a couple of seats. Remove these, and we have all the space we want. With three or four stretchers and mattresses, with proper bed furniture to match, a dozen yards of ten cent muslin to make rollers, a little linen and lint, a couple of rolls of cotton batting, a yard of strapping, a few square feet of thin hard pine, a small saw to cut it up with, a stone bottle for hot water, and a tourniquet or two, which any conductor can be easily taught to apply; adding, perhaps, a little brandy, a small bottle of laudanum, and one of hartshorn—we shall have provision, such as would not only allow a conductor to perform the first requisites, but to enable a moderately efficient medical man, should there be one in the cars, which is often the case, to put up a patient in a comfortable manner until he was in a situation to be placed under permanent treatment; or, at least, in charge of a district surgeon, who might live at a considerable distance from the scene of the accident. For instance, suppose a brakeman, or passenger, stepping from one car to another, fell from the platform and sustained a severe fracture, with other injuries; the conductor, if there were much hæmorrhage, could apply a tourniquet, place him in a comfortable position on a mattress, apply a warm water bottle to his feet, and so carry him, with little disturbance, until delivered to the surgeon who was to treat him. If a medical man happened to be in the cars, he might, in addition, pillow the limb, or use splint or bandage, or administer restoratives, or an opiate, as the circumstances of the case warranted in his judgment. In other respects, the same principles and mode of proceeding would apply as heretofore laid down. The car, containing the above requisites, should be as near to the centre of the train as possible, as least liable to injury. One or other of the above named provisions, or both combined, would suffice to meet the wants of every railroad in existence. In the case of short lines of railroad, not exceeding twenty or thirty miles, an inspector would be unnecessary, requiring only provision in the cars, and a surgeon at either end. Where a short line is leased to a great main road, the medical arrangements of the lesser would be merged in those of the greater.

Such is the basis I propose for a general system of medical provision for railroads. It would be out of place here to enter into the nature of the instructions and regulations that would issue from the inspector's office for the guidance of his staff, further than to say that they would probably resolve themselves into two kinds: first, such as might be suggested by the superintendent as necessary to bring the whole working arrangements of the line into harmony; and second, advisory as relating to new discoveries in science, new principles of treatment, new appliances, or whatever may seem calculated to promote our efficiency as practitioners. An institution so extensive cannot be expected to start into existence in full perfection, though all our main ends will be secured from the commencement. After a little working of the machinery all asperities will be smoothed down, and a system as perfect and beautiful in all its parts as combined talent and skill can make it will soon result.

A word with regard to our profession. We shall here have a great number of intelligent professional minds enlisted and immediately interested in the work. From such many excellent practical suggestions will emanate, which, gradually embodied into rules and regulations within the capacity of employees, will tend to perfect the general system and increase its efficiency. Should the medical officers of a line come together once a year bringing reports of cases and the results of their experiences, accustomed as they would be to treat desperate injuries, we might look for much tending to advance general professional knowledge. Whatever proved of eminent utility in one case would become the common property of all, and might at stated interva's be embodied in circulars, which would be interchanged with similar ones issued by the officers of other lines. In most neighborhoods efficient medical men will be found. There may, however, be some localities newly settled and sparsely populated, where good surgeons, if any at all, are difficult to be found. In such places there are often influential men, who are selected as directors of the line which passes through them. Let these look around, select from among the more distinguished young graduates of our great medical schools competent men for their district surgeons, give them enough of the family patronage and that of their friends to enable them to live at the start, and they will gradually become the consulting surgeons of their neighborhood, introducing a higher standard of local professional attainment, as well as helping to elevate and ennoble our profession in the minds of the people generally.

A few words must suffice, as not properly belonging here, with regard to the economy to railroads generally in adopting a system of medical provision. I have already alluded to the diminution of litigation, and check to fraudulent actions, by the command, on the part of railroads, of medical witnesses, who had been enabled to examine every injured person at the time of the accident. To this must be added the diminished liability of the companies, which will be in proportion to the life-saving efficiency of the arrangements proposed. In the statements of expenses for 1860, in the State Engineer's Report, we find under the head of " Damages to Passengers," on the five railroads previously mentioned, the sum of $50,706 (I omit cents), of which $33,626 were paid by a single corporation, although only nine passengers were killed and forty-three injured ; while another paid only $12,366, with eighteen passengers killed and forty-three injured ; a third paid $1,241, with twenty passengers killed and forty-six injured ; and again with a fourth, $3,223 are registered against a company with no passengers on the killed and injured list. This part of our statistics, therefore, affords no uniformity in its results, as might be expected, where two or three years may elapse on a line without any very great accident, although when one of the latter does occur, the damages may amply compensate by their amount for the smallness of them in other years. Taking an average of the amount paid by the five alluded to previously, in 1860, it will be a little over ten thousand dollars for each. On some lines no accidents are recorded under any head. On sixteen lines where such have occurred, with a total length of 1,954 miles, the total amount of damages paid for injuries to passengers was $60,725, a little over $3,100 for every hundred miles of road. In other years of course the statements will vary, some paying more, some less. Some will meet with heavy accidents where none have heretofore occurred, and others will be comparatively free from them, which now figure heavily in the list. As with the advent of epidemics, there is no certainty about them, except that they will certainly turn up somewhere or other. Let them not find us unprepared.

Of the thirteen hundred and seven persons killed and injured, and heretofore alluded to, we find that six hundred and eighty-seven belonged to the companies, either as passengers or employees, while six hundred and twenty, or nearly one-half of the whole number, were persons unconnected in any way with the respective lines, and for whose injuries the companies cannot for the most part be held in any way responsible. They cannot, nevertheless, be overlooked in any humane endeavors for the relief of the injured. True, many of these are killed instantly by being run over or struck by the engine ; but still a very large number remains, and this leads to the irresistible inference, that while the companies should be compelled to do their duty in this matter, there is also a large part to be performed by the public themselves, upon whose shoulders a portion of the burden should justly rest. Let, therefore, the railroad managers provide their stations or surgeons, paying the latter for the first dressing, at least, in all cases, and giving to all a share in their life-saving arrangement, whether connected with the line or not. Let, on the other hand, the public establish societies on the same principles of benevolence as those for the saving of life by any other class of casualties, calling them Railroad Accident

Relief Societies, or by any other name they please, whose object it would be to strengthen the hands of surgeons by furnishing stations and flag stations with needful apparatus, such as the stretchers, bedding, and bed-furniture, splints, and those necessaries which no individual practitioner could be expected to possess in sufficient quantity to meet the requirements of a great accident. Of these the inspectors of lines might be made the distributing agents. As passengers and employees would share in the advantages offered thereby to others, the companies would thus get a fair *quid pro quo.*

When the companies have done all in their power—and as far as judicious regulations, and careful and vigilant supervision go, I believe they have—to insure the safety of those who travel on their lines, and have further by proper arrangements done their best for the recovery of those who may be injured, thus making complete provision for every emergency in every department, they will have a good right to claim at the hands of their respective legislatures, relief by the introduction of measures of limited liability. As the laws stand at present, I believe it is sometimes cheaper to kill people outright than merely to hurt them. They should not be made to pay more for lives saved than for lives lost. To railroad managers these propositions are respectfully submitted. Let them once take into serious consideration the question, whether the claims of humanity and the interests of stockholders are not entirely reconcilable in this matter, and the ultimate result cannot be doubtful.

To return to my legitimate sphere. I have in this paper devoted more space to the necessity for medical provision for railroads, than to the details of it; for, let but the truths I have here endeavored to lay down be established in principle, the necessity for action in the matter of railroad accidents be once fairly impressed on the public mind, and we may rest assured that, based either on my plans or some better ones, a great and noble institution will ere long start into existence; the result of which will be to save as much life, to alleviate as much suffering, as any one of the great benevolent institutions of the day. We must not, in this or any other new and great undertaking, expect perfection at the start. There will be many practical difficulties to surmount, requiring in any one who shall be entrusted with the task of putting the scheme into practical operation, talent, energy, and entire devotion to the work before him. We should have to decide exactly before going to expense what apparatus we would employ, and, in some instances, adopt new contrivances. Abundance of surgical apparatus we have; but bearing in mind that our arrangements are but for temporary purposes; that everything must be reduced to the smallest amount of space compatible with the object to be attained, as well as to be of the most portable kind; that cheapness, too, will be an essential matter; we shall have to look forward to many new and simpler appliances than those often in use in permanently treating a case. For instance, the most important piece of furniture would be the hand ambulance. Now, I think it would be easy to construct a thing of this kind, which, folded up, would form a simple flat stretcher; the legs dropping from the sides, it would form a bedstead; and by curtain posts, that might be raised up from either end, the curtains being usually kept folded under the mattress, convertible into a covered hand ambulance; so that from the moment a patient was taken up and laid on the stretcher, whether he were conveyed to a station, or put into a car or carried through the streets, he would never have to be disturbed from his original recumbent position until placed under the care of the surgeon destined permanently to attend him. In this, and similar matters, with able inspectors, willing to listen to every suggestion, and capable of sifting the chaff from the wheat, and determined to adopt nothing that was not thoroughly practical, as well as reasonably economical; with a large body of able practitioners associated directly in the work, and the general intelligence of the whole mass of the profession to guide and assist them, all obstacles, as far as our part was concerned, would be easily surmounted.

I had now arrived at the concluding paragraph of my paper, when I received an important communication bearing, immediately on the subject in question. Singularly enough, while I was working out the above details, another gentleman was preparing a great and comprehensive measure now ready to go before the legislature with the sanction and support of most of the leading Railroad Presidents, as I am informed, and of which this very medical provision forms an essential feature. It is only within the last few days that either party has been aware of the proceedings of the other, yet the two measures dovetail into each other exactly, the one clearing away all financial difficulties, the other supplying a basis for the proposed surgical attendance. I am permitted to give an abstract of the proposed measure.

[As several modifications were made in the Bill since this paper was read, and as in the next article a full abstract is given of the measure as it stands at present, I omit it here.]

In view of the fact that the question of medical provision for railroads is about to come up before the Legislature of the State in a measure thus large and comprehensive, would it not be desirable that this Society should take some action in the premises by a petition to the Legislature setting forth that, in the opinion of this body, great suffering is entailed and much loss of life and limb incurred by the want of medical provision calculated to secure more speedy and efficient attendance on persons injured by railroad accidents, and praying that the legislative body will either originate some measure or take into their earnest consideration such as may be brought before them bearing on the subject, in order that thereby the desired object of proper medical provision for railroads may be ultimately secured by such legislative enactments as in their wisdom may seem proper. I am not in the habit of drawing up petitions; but by such a one, you would, and none could do it with more propriety as representatives of the great medical body of the State, without interfering with functions not properly belonging to you, be the first to step forward as promoters and pioneers of a great and humane movement.

In conclusion, when our object shall be finally attained, we have only to do our whole duty, leaving the rest in the hands of an all-wise, overruling Providence. Successful, we shall carry joy into many a household that might otherwise have been made desolate: should it be differently ordered, though we fail to save life, we shall not fail to diminish suffering; the last moments of the unfortunate sufferer will not be embittered by unnecessary torture, and what can by possibility be avoided is unnecessary; while to sorrowing and perhaps distant relatives there will be afforded the one source of consolation that all had been done by wise precautions and humane provision, as well as by practical sympathy and professional skill, that could reasonably be looked for in an enlightened and Christian community.

YONKERS, *February* 1, 1862.

ACTION TAKEN BY THE NEW YORK MEDICAL SOCIETY.

The following report of the Proceedings is taken from the American Medical Times.

" Dr. Shrady (N. Y.), offered a preamble and resolution relative to the medical provision for railroads, as advocated by Dr. Arnold during the morning session :—

" *Whereas*, In the opinion of this Society, much loss of life and limb occur from want of sufficiently speedy medical assistance in cases of railroad accidents, and

" *Whereas*, The efforts of medical men, when present, are often rendered nugatory by the want of suitable appliances, and

3

" *Whereas,* It is desirable that some better provision should be made than at present exists to prevent railroad casualties, and

" *Whereas,* The Society has been informed that a large and comprehensive measure is about to be introduced into the Legislature of the State, of which proper medical attendance for railroads forms an essential feature : therefore be it

" *Resolved,* That a Committee be appointed to report at the earliest moment whether any or what action shall be taken by this Society in the premises.

" The Committee consisted of Drs. G. F. Shrady, E. Arnold, and A. Willard, of Chenango."

At the morning session, on the following day : " Dr. Shrady, as Chairman of the Committee to report on medical provision for railroads, offered the following for adoption :—

" *Whereas,* This Society has heard that a measure is about being introduced into the Senate, of which an essential feature is thorough medical provision for railroads, and

" *Whereas,* We believe that much loss of life and limb result from want of such provisions : therefore be it

" *Resolved,* That we hail with satisfaction the introduction of any plans calculated to secure so desirable an end, and

" *Resolved,* That a copy of the foregoing be forwarded to Senator Smith, of Kings county, the gentleman who has given notice to the Senate of the introduction of such a measure."

The foregoing Preamble and Resolutions were duly seconded and unanimously adopted.

MEDICAL PROVISION FOR RAILROADS.

SUPPLEMENTARY PAPER:

CONTAINING ALSO AN ANALYSIS OF THE BILL ENTITLED

A BILL to provide Compensation to Passengers for Injuries sustained
on the Railroads of the State; also to provide Surgical Stations
and Hospital Accommodations on the Railroads of the State.

Read before the Surgical Section of the New York
Academy of Medicine, October 24, 1862,

By E. S. F. ARNOLD, M.D., M.R.C.S.E.,

RESIDENT FELLOW OF THE ACADEMY.

THE need of some arrangements better than those now exist-
ing for the saving of life in cases of railway casualty has been
so generally admitted by medical men; so many, both in and
out of the profession, have not only endorsed the propriety of
measures to that effect, but expressed a wonder that such had
not been suggested before, that it would be a waste of time to
bring before this body any fresh arguments to prove the necessity of medical provision for railroads.

It will be remembered that on the 28th of February last, I
was called upon to explain my views, of which the following
may be regarded as a summary :—The attachment to our leading stations, at intervals, where practicable, of not more than
ten miles, of a small room kept at all times in readiness for the
reception of injured persons, and providing the same with surgical apparatus, carrying also appliances in the cars where the
stations were too far apart to enable us to get at such apparatus without great loss of time. The appointment of competent
surgeons to attend to the injured, unpaid, but payable for actual
services rendered ; such services to extend, however, only to
such a period as shall enable sufferers to be removed without
risk to the care of their own medical attendant, or be otherwise safely disposed of. The District surgeon would also take
authoritative charge in case of any great accident involving
injury to a number, seeing to it that all were efficiently cared
for, to effect which he would be empowered not only to avail
himself of any efficient medical assistance at hand, but also to

call in additional aid, if necessary. The appointment, lastly, of a general medical superintendent to supervise the working of the whole.

By the adoption of such arrangements, with their attendant details, I claim, not only that the loss of much life and limb would be avoided, but that, in cases where thus much could not be accomplished, we should at least be enabled greatly to mitigate the sufferings of the victims of railway casualty. I claim also, as railroads are becoming the great vehicle of travel in every part of the world, and inasmuch as with the best of care and regulations, wood and iron will give out at the high rates of speed required and attained, that the proposed institution, once introduced and incorporated into the railway system, could take its place by the side of the other great humanitarian life-saving institutions of the age, while, as regards expense, it would ere long be rather a source of economy, than otherwise, to adopt such measures.

One of the medical journals (*Phil. Med. & Surg. Reporter*), in a very complimentary article upon my former paper, asks, however: "whether the plan proposed is not more complicated than necessary, and whether the end sought could not be attained by less machinery? whether the impromptu gathering of surgeons from the vicinity where an accident occurs, their compensation to be regulated in the same manner as that for other services rendered and to be paid by the company, would not be much more simple, prompt, and effective, and comport better with the dignity of the profession? Whether, if the surgical appliances are kept, as they should be, at stations and in the trains, as a part of the paraphernalia of the road, the end sought, viz. the speedy care of the wounded and mutilated, and the speedy supply of all their necessities, could not be better accomplished without the routine of 'Head Surgeon' and 'District Surgeon,' general duties and subordinate duties?" The paragraph just quoted may serve as a text to say a few words on the administrative features of the proposed system, which have been only lightly touched upon in my former paper.

When a person is seriously injured by railroad casualty he is often perfectly frantic to be removed to his friends, although perhaps a long distance from home, and why? Partly, no doubt, because he has more confidence in his own medical adviser than in strangers; partly, because there is a strong natural desire to be amongst one's own friends when life is in danger; but is this all? I think a more powerful motive still comes into play, viz. the dread of falling into incompetent hands. This it is that mainly induces him to wish removal to a great distance when he feels that he needs quiet and rest; and if he knew of a well-appointed hospital in the neighborhood, I feel sure that in nine cases out of ten he would say—"Carry me there." By the establishment simply of hospital stations we should make some approach to this, but without regularly appointed medical men we should not be much better off than before. We should have all the expense with but a small portion of the advantages resulting from adoption of the entire plan. Under the proposed system the railroad employees would know exactly where to look for the most competent surgeon in any given neigborhood, which is seldom the case at present, and a general knowledge of the fact would tend greatly to add to the feeling of security on the part of travellers. Again, what could more forcibly illustrate the necessity of some one competent man taking charge in case of many being injured than the scene described by a distinguished member of your own body, at a former meeting of this section, when summoned to a great accident; where regu'ar practitioners, homœopaths, hydropaths, Thompsonians, and herb doctors all rushed to the spot, and whoever could first stick a piece of plaster upon one of the unfortunate victims of his attention claimed him as his patient, adding thereby only to the prevailing confusion, and accomplishing nothing, so that he was finally compelled to take the whole in charge. Would the system I have proposed be worth a straw, if every practitioner, whether regular or irregular, were considered competent to carry it out in its most important particular—the affording prompt and efficient relief to the injured? Is the selection of skilled members of the profession of less importance than the choice of apparatus? How would it be with our public hospitals if every one who signs M.D. to his name were, without reference to special qualifications, considered competent and voted in or appointed as interest might dictate? Are skill and judgment less called for when a man is so mutilated that his life hangs upon a thread? No, gentlemen, I think you will agree with me, that the selection of the best talent to be had is the first and greatest requisite of our scheme. Hence I regard the appointment of district surgeons as a necessity to the public. There is another point of view interesting more particularly to practitioners themselves. If we are to have efficient medical provision for railroads there must be a better understanding between practitioners and railroad men, and to accomplish this it must be grafted in as a part of the general system. At present when an accident occurs medical men are called at random, by whom nobody knows, and on arriving are without authority to enforce their wishes, and are sometimes even denied requisite information; the officials fear to commit themselves, and regard the surgeon almost as an interloper, certainly treat him as such, and finally throw the case on his hands to do the best he can with it. Of course, nobody is responsible to him, if the patient is not capable of doing anything, and a just feeling of discontent is engendered. These things, it is true, lie out of the sphere of general observation, but they create ill-feeling and a dislike often to have anything to do with railroad accidents, if they can avoid it. I believe with the introduction of the system I have proposed all these difficulties will be easily obviated. The district surgeon, while on duty, would be an officer of the line, bound to do his best for the relief of sufferers, and entitled to the same respect and consideration as any other superior employee in enforcing what he deemed necessary; while, on the other hand, he would be the local guardian of the interests of the company, as far as his own department was concerned.

If railroad companies were to attempt to put a system of medical provision into operation with their present machinery, they would simply undertake an impossibility. Stations might be established, but when it came to determining the nature of apparatus to be employed, and supplying the stations with requisites, they would be at a standstill. There would be abundance of communications, the value of which non-professional men could not estimate, and almost every practitioner would want something different. The time of superintendents would be so trespassed upon with questions beyond their power to determine, that the necessity of some medical man at head-quarters to take charge of the whole matter would soon be apparent; hence, while the district-surgeon would be a necessity to the public, a medical superintendent would be indispensable to the companies, alike on the score of time, trouble, and expense. Doubly so would this be the case, if the companies of a State were to associate themselves as proposed in the Bill I shall presently have occasion to introduce to your notice. By that measure not less than a hundred and fifty stations are contemplated in this State. The two grand features of the proposal are Life Insurance and Medical provision; and as the latter is most novel, most prominent, most difficult to carry out, the chief executive officer, call him Superintendent, Medical Inspector, Surgeon-in-chief, or what you will, must be a medical man. His duties would be entirely different from those of the district surgeons, and mainly administrative. Here is a scheme to be so grafted on to the railway system, that while novel and great facilities are to be afforded to the profession to relieve suffering humanity, no derangement of the ordinary working machinery, no detriment to the interests of companies shall thereby occur. When we have determined upon our apparatus, similar in character for each and every station, and fixed upon the latter, and districts and surgeons, and the whole is put into operation, it must be evident to every thinking mind, that there are still a great many small matters of detail to be worked out, ere the machinery of one blends into that of the other, so as to form one harmonious whole. For instance, instructions to employees must not be such as will interfere with their other duties—we must not risk the safety of a train to assist an individual. The rights and privileges of medical officers must be so defined, that, while every facility is thereby secured to them for the most prompt and efficient discharge of their functions, they shall not be brought into conflict with other employees. Again, with regard to payments of medical men, the companies or association must know exactly what they are going to do. They make themselves responsible for payment in cases where they are not now legally so; they extend their humane provision to ALL cases of casualty on their lines, and the profession must meet them half way. The duties to be performed are specific, and extend only over a short period, hence there will be no difficulty in placing these things upon a fixed basis, otherwise, while all legal difficulties are obviated, as between companies and their passengers, new ones would soon spring up between the former and practitioners. These and similar matters are within the compass of any ordinarily clear-headed practitioner to arrange as they arise, but they must be presented in a well-digested form to the general superintendents of lines, whose labors are already incessant and arduous enough, and whose time ought not to be trenched upon unnecessarily by matters out of their respective lines of duty. There will be enough to occupy the whole time and attention of the chief medical officer where the system is perfected. Placed as he is between the profession, whose just wishes he will of course be anxious to respond to, and the companies whose interests in this matter are placed in his charge, his duties will be partly secretarial. There will be a considerable amount of correspondence with the parties between whom he stands. He will supply and have charge of all apparatus, and should inspect every station at least once a year; should be on hand, if possible, after every great accident, and watch the working of the system, and see how the duties are performed; he should also embody an account of the labors of railroad surgeons in a comprehensive annual report. There will be too much for him to do to be compatible with anything like remunerative private practice; enough to fill his whole time, which at all events must be paid for, advantageously to his employers. Upon his activity and energy much of the success of the plan will depend; and at least until the system is in complete working order, he will have, if he would avoid general confusion and ultimate disappointment, to bend his whole energies to the task.

There is nothing here really about head surgeon and district surgeon, or general duties and subordinate duties. There is nothing to interfere with the freest action of local surgeons. When occasion occurs they would be authorized to go ahead at once, with facilities placed at their command they do not now possess; and having done their work and made their report they would be entitled to and receive their pay without any question arising as to the responsibility or non-responsibility of the company on whose line the accident occurred.

I should propose that the report so made should be on a printed formula, to be kept at all stations and include the following inquiries :—As to the distance from the station and time at which the accident occurred : what was done previous to the arrival of the surgeon : the time the patient arrived at the station, and length of time that elapsed before he was put under treatment : the exact nature of his injuries, the treatment and results : if dying, specifying the time and immediate cause of death ; if living, how disposed of. These reports filed and bound would make a most valuable statistical record, and would enable us to test with great exactness the success or non-success of our scheme. I shall now take leave of this part of my subject, merely remarking, that whatever of complexity there may seem to be about it, will disappear as soon as it is put into practical working shape. As with all other new and great measures, unless reduced to system, this would soon become surrounded with difficulties, and end in failure.

With regard to *apparatus*—I have already indicated, in a general manner, in my former paper, the kind we should require. Every surgeon who is qualified to undertake the duties of district surgeon will be expected to possess as many instruments at least as are comprised in Tiemann's forty dollar case, if only to meet the exigencies of his private practice ; we need not therefore supply cutting instruments. Neither is it to be supposed that we can supply to stations all the resources of large and well appointed hospitals. Country surgeons are, from the necessities of their position, often obliged, in cases of fracture, whether simple or compound, to make their splints on the spot. Some adopt one contrivance, some another, especially to meet the exigency of the moment ; and as Ferguson has well observed : "More after all depends on the skill and care of the surgeon than on the employment of any particular kind of apparatus." All we could do would be to supply the rough material. Stretchers would be supplied to the minor or flag stations; the main stations would of course be better provided.

As this subject may not come up again, I shall beg to introduce to your notice an apparatus specially suited for removal of a difficult class of cases, namely, those with fractures of the thigh. It is a fracture bed, invented by Dr. Robert Nelson, formerly of Canada, and now of this city. It is on the double inclined plane principle, and so constructed that the leg operates as the extending weight. By this apparatus the Doctor claims to treat fractures without splints, and when properly used, without a possibility of shortening. As he has determined to make this apparatus public, and has already given notice of a paper to be read by him on the subject, in the Medico-Chirurgical Society, it would be out of place here to do more than merely exhibit it, he having kindly given me permission to do so. On the bed from which this model was taken, I have treated one patient with perfect success, and without splints a great part of the time. What is still more to the purpose, at present I have put a man with fractured thigh upon it, without a splint or support of any kind, pushed the whole on a common express cart, during Christmas week, when the roads were rough, and so sent him down without experiencing (as he expressed it) an ache, or a jar, or a pain, from the time he left Yonkers until he was delivered at his destination. He might as well have been carried to New Orleans. I have added handles and curtains, and the whole is compact and portable. A dozen or so might be distributed in central locations, so that on requisition by telegraph one or more could be easily forwarded to any locality where it might be needed. [The apparatus was here exhibited and described; one of the main objects being to show how an injured person might have the limb set at the station, be thence removed to a hotel, again to the cars, through the streets, or home to any distance, without disturbance, without removing him from the bed, or altering his position.]

I have advocated the measure now under discussion as a *source of economy* to companies; of course, during the first year or two there would be an increase of expense, but the stations once fitted up, and apparatus supplied, both would last for many years. There are about 2,650 miles of railroad worked by locomotives in this State. I propose that during the first year ten dollars per mile should be allowed for fitting of stations, and ten more for apparatus, which would amount to $53,000;

half of that amount, perhaps, for the next year, and for several years subsequently nothing at all. The general medical expenses, exclusive of superintendence, would probably not exceed one dollar per mile, or $2,650 per annum. The total cost of medical provision, if carried out on this scale, would be for the first year about $2,300 per hundred miles, including supervision and medical attendance, $1,300 on second year, and subsequently not exceed $350 per annum for a number of years. This is supposing the railroads to be associated. If going separately to work it would cost them much more for apparatus and superintendence. The total cost to the companies for damages to persons in 1860 was $59,064, or at the rate of $2.223 and a fraction for every hundred miles, and in 1861 $52,727, or $2.361 and a fraction for every hundred miles. The average in other years would be, probably, not far from these figures. This part of my subject will be, perhaps, more intelligible if we take a single line of railroad, say the Hudson River Railroad, giving the length of it in round numbers at 150 miles. Its share of the expense, on the associated plan, would be, for the first year, $3,450, for the second $1,950, and for several subsequent years not over $525 per annum. The amount of damages for injuries to persons paid by this Company in 1861, according to the State Engineer's Report for that year [the latest I have been able to obtain], was $33,626. This, however, as we see by the above statement, is far above the average, an accident of unusual severity having occurred; but, making every allowance for this, it must be evident, that it would need but small success of the above scheme not only to cover the entire outlay, but even to effect a saving to the Company.

Before entering upon the second part of my subject, I wish to be allowed to say a few words, which though of purely personal interest now, may, perhaps, be one of inquiry hereafter. Two parties have proposed this medical provision, have put forward measures distinct in themselves, but blending so together as to constitute really but one, and both claim, I have no doubt justly, entire originality. As to myself, my mind has been quietly occupied with it for several years, each case of railroad injury that has occurred in the vicinity, and to which I have been summoned, bringing up the question more and more forcibly. Various schemes presented themselves and were rejected as impracticable. At last it seemed to resolve itself into a shape in which conflicting interests might be reconciled, and I wrote, now more than eighteen months since, to one of our most prominent railway directors, embodying, substantially, the same propositions I afterwards brought forward. Not receiving any answer, the subject again fell to the ground for the time. Finally, it seemed a duty to bring it more prominently forward, and I ventured to send the " letter of a country surgeon" to the American "Medical Times." This meeting with a favorable reception, I republished it, with additions, in small pamphlet form, the whole of which also appeared in one of our local papers on the first of January last, and sent it out as a feeler, if I may so express it, to medical men, lawyers and merchants of my acquaintance with a like encouraging result. In doubt whether to let the matter rest there, or go forward and bring it before the State Medical Society, I now determined to consult our venerable friend Dr. Valentine Mott, and to rely entirely on his advice as to my future course. He strongly recommended me to go on. This was in the middle of January, and in another week my paper for the State Medical Society was written. When commencing it I had addressed a note to the Secretary of the Hudson River Railroad, asking for a copy of their annual report. He was absent at the time, but on the 21st of January, sent a reply, referring me to the State Engineer, and added the following paragraph: "I also write to say that Mr. N. D. Morgan, of this city (residing at Irvington), is engaged in preparing and urging a law in relation to accidents on railroads, which is to embrace in its provisions somewhat such an arrangement of surgical stations on every railroad as is embraced in the pamphlet you sent me. · It might be well for you to talk with him on the subject." A few days later I had the pleasure of meeting Mr. Morgan and of becoming acquainted with his plans, and since then we have worked together.

I now proceed to the consideration of the Bill on file in the State Senate, of which I gave an abstract in my former paper, and in so doing abandon original ground. I claim neither part nor lot in this, as it appears to me, admirable legislative measure, and shall use indiscriminately the arguments employed by Mr. Morgan or myself, as developed in our mutual correspondence, leaving the entire credit, as it justly belongs, to himself. Several alterations having been made in it during its passage through the Special Committee to which it was referred, the details will necessarily differ somewhat from those in the former statement.

" *The Bill to provide Compensation to Passengers for personal injury received on the Railroads of the State, and for the establishment of Surgical Stations and Hospital Accommodations on the Railroads of the State,*"
was introduced by Senator Smith, of Kings county, on the 5th of February last, and on the following day referred to the In-

surance Committee. Its main provisions in its present state are
as follows :

It provides for an association of the railroad companies of
the State, the same to be a " body corporate," managed by a
"Board of Managers," consisting of the Presidents, or such
other officers of the associa'ed companies, as may be designated
by the respective companies, and the President of the association, who shall be a citizen of the State of New York, and not
an officer of any railroad company.

The association shall make up a guarantee fund of $100,000,
chargeable upon each road as to its passenger traffic ; and to
enable the association of railroads to meet casualties, the respective companies shall, in their discretion, be allowed to charge
four-tenths of a mill per mile to every passenger, or one cent
for every twenty-five miles or distance within it, in addition to
the usual fare. In return for this, each passenger is guaranteed,
in case of death, $5,000 to his heirs ; in case of loss of a limb,
or an incurable injury seriously interfering with usual occupa-
tions, $5,000, and for minor injuries $25 per week, provided
that such payments shall not extend over fifty-two weeks. The
association also undertakes to establish surgical stations, at distances of not over ten miles from any one spot, which shall be
provided with suitable necessaries, and to appoint competent
surgeons to attend them when required. This done, the railroad
companies are to be exempted from all liability on account of
any accident to passengers.

The bill provides further, that the fund raised by the tax
upon passengers, which may be called the " Casualty Fund,"
shall be employed for no other purpose than to pay compensations with the necessary expenses of management, and that
whatever remains over and above shall accumulate, and when
the interest on such accumulation shall amount to a sum equal
to the tax of one-tenth of a mill, then the tax on the public
shall be reduced to three-tenths of a mill, and so on until the
passenger tax is abolished altogether. The medical provision
will be paid for by other means, to be presently mentioned.

I may here observe that there is one point, on which I differ slightly from the author of the measure. He proposes that
surgical stations should not be further than ten miles from any
one spot. This would contemplate stations twenty miles apart.
I propose that they should not be more than ten, and that where
this is not practicable we should make some provision in the
cars. Suppose that two given stations were twenty miles apart
and an accident happened five miles beyond one of them, the
train could not go back to the nearest one, and it would have
to carry the sufferer fifteen miles, often with great delay from

intermediate stoppages. Such distance ought to be reduced to a minimum. Ten mile distances absolutely between stations would be far more appropriate, and not involve too great an outlay. The more thorough the provision the greater the ultimate economy both of life and money.

To return to the Bill—it provides that on an accident occurring on any road, the company shall be fined to the extent of one-third of the amount to which it has rendered the associated fund liable. This fine is to go into a special fund which may be called the "Reward and Penalty" fund. For instance, if five passengers were killed and others injured so as between them to draw for five thousand more on the casualty fund, and the total thereby made $30,000, the company, on whose line the accident occurred, would pay $10,000 into the reward and penalty fund. Thus, while whatever comes from the public will go back to the public, on the other hand, the companies are by no means relieved from liability. Owing to the liberal compensations allowed, the penalty would in many cases be greater than that now entailed through the instrumentality of courts of law.

A clause has likewise been introduced by which, when companies send sufferers to hospitals, and pay usual rates for attendance on the same, such action shall not be held to imply any legal liability for damages on the part of the company.—The object of this is as follows : when a person is injured and sent by the railroad company to an unendowed hospital, it (the company) is willing to pay the same as others for the attendance, but insists that a paper shall be signed by the injured person to the effect that doing so shall not be held as an admission of culpability on its own part. No sooner are such persons in the hospital than they are surrounded by a low class of lawyers, who persuade them not to sign any such paper, and consequently companies are compelled to refuse payment for their own protection. The difficulty is obviated by the above clause.

Out of the reward and penalty fund all charges of medical provision and general hospital expenses are to be paid, and at the end of the fiscal year whatever remains over and above is to be redistributed among all the companies pro rata as to their contribution to the casualty fund. Thus, as Mr. Morgan observes, "rewards and penalties are set forth of the highest importance, as securing care and proper equipment on every road of the association." Companies not meeting with any accidents will be absolute gainers, while those with whom they occur will foot all the expenses.

Such are the main provisions of the Bill, and it appears to me that, based, as the measure is, partly upon life insurance principles, partly on purely humane considerations, substantial justice is rendered to every class. While passengers are taxed only to compensate passengers, the companies extend their provision to EVERY class of the injured, and thereby inaugurate a truly great humanitarian institution.

I have shown, in my former paper, that the expense of medical provision should not fall entirely on the railroad companies, inasmuch as the majority of injured persons are hurt through their own carelessness, or disregard of rules and regulations, so as to absolve the companies from all legal liability. Although it is borne by the companies in this Bill, yet, their responsibility being lessened in other ways, they cannot complain ; on the other hand, as the parties most interested are those who travel, the proposed arrangements being mainly for their benefit, and as in case of accident not only will they be more speedily attended to, but damages promptly paid without recourse to expensive litigation, a tax so slight as not to be felt by any one, yet securing such desirable objects, ought not to excite discontent—they receive a full quid pro quo.

It has been urged, that as railroad companies are wealthy corporations, privileged nominally for the public benefit, but carried on practically for their own, they are rich enough and morally bound, even when not legally so, to make such provision themselves. In this matter Mr. Morgan claims, that his Bill charging every passenger four-tenths of a mill extra fare, is based upon the theory, that our railroad companies cannot afford to pay compensation for injury and for proper care of the injured out of the sum now exacted from passengers. Taking the passenger traffic on the roads of the State of New York for 1860, it is found that a dividend of $5_{\frac{2}{10}}$ths per cent. on the paid up capital stock was earned ; this, however, was not paid, as a portion of this was expended in construction. If we take the entire traffic of all the roads in the State, it appears that they have only earned a dividend of $3_{\frac{56}{100}}$ths per cent. Now what can be expected from stockholders under such circumstances? Will they spend money in making their roads safe, or in compensating for broken limbs? No, they will trust to luck rather than forego a dividend, and that not because they entertain a more than usual disregard for human life, but simply because they are human, and such low state of finances tends to such results. If it is clear that the railroads do not receive sufficient fare to provide safe transit, and to compensate those who may be injured on their roads, will not our Legislature grant the privilege to the roads of collecting, while they bear a fair share of the burden, such additional fare as will be sufficient to meet all the demands upon roads for casualties? "My plan," Mr.

Morgan says, "is after all but a mutual insurance by all the railroad companies against the possibility of large losses. The large roads will contribute to the fund, which is to protect a small road from loss too much for a small road to bear under the present system. My plan covers this and much more, for it gives compensation certain and sufficient for the hazard of travel by rail; it saves life and suffering by its surgical provision; it is promotive of a better feeling between railroad companies and the public. They are mutually interested in the welfare of the road and the safety of the passenger."

I will allude only to one other objection that might be raised. Many, leaving out of view the collateral advantages altogether, might look upon this as a mere life insurance system, and object to it, inasmuch as the companies are compelled by law to pay full damages for injuries sustained on their roads. Is this really so? Are damages granted as liberal as the compensation here allowed? Are they ever paid without recourse to long and tedious legislation? Do not parties often fail to fasten legal responsibility on the companies after battling for years through every court in the State? I think we shall have to admit that the law courts are but a tedious and uncertain resource at best. Mr. Morgan quotes, as a case in point, that of a young woman lately injured, resulting in the loss of a foot, and where a verdict of $3000 was given. This was deemed too much by the road, and a new trial was to be had, and it is possibly not settled yet, and may not be for a long time to come, nor, if it is the same as in many other cases, until all benefit to the sufferer has died out in costs. Under the proposed system, every passenger is paid for injury, if injured while on his passage from causes incidental to railroad travelling—no questions are asked.

It appears to me that the measure, of which I have detailed the principal features, taken in its entirety, is one as noble in its objects as it is comprehensive in its details; and I am happy to be able to add that it has some good friends in the Legislature. Having passed through special committee, it is now on file in the Senate, and will, I am informed, be brought up at an early period of the next session.

Not doubting that you will feel interested in the success of the legislative measure, the subject is nevertheless too new to you to warrant me in asking any expression of opinion on it as a whole. As relates, however, to the propriety of medical provision for railroads, that has now been long before you. I shall therefore beg leave, in concluding, to propose a set of resolutions somewhat similar to those adopted by the State Medical Society:

1st. That in the opinion of this body the loss of many lives would be avoided, and a great diminution of suffering brought about by the adoption of a system of local medical provision on our railroads to meet the cases of casualty occurring thereon.

2d. That such a medical provision could readily be made by fitting up a small room at main stations, and at distances not more than ten miles apart, where practicable, for temporary hospital purposes, and by providing the same with suitable apparatus, and appointing a competent surgeon in the neighborhood to attend on call as occasion may arise.

3d. That, when important stations are too far apart to admit of such an arrangement, suitable apparatus should be carried in the cars themselves, and stations be established where the most competent practitioners of surgery are to be found.

4th. That as we have been informed of the existence of a measure before the Legislature of the State, entitled : " A Bill to provide compensation to passengers for personal injury received on the railroads of the State, and for the establishment of surgical stations and hospital accommodations on the railroads of the State ;" therefore, that a copy of the above resolutions be forwarded to the Senators of this county, and that they be urgently requested to lay the same before the Senate when the above measure, or any other embracing like surgical provision, may come up, full as such provisions are of life-saving efficacy in this age of general railroad travel, and the consequent loss of life and limb entailed by the casualties occurring from time to time on railroads.

YONKERS, *October*, 1862.

ACTION OF THE SURGICAL SECTION OF THE NEW YORK ACADEMY OF MEDICINE.

On publishing my first small pamphlet, consisting of the "Letter of a Country Surgeon, with preface and postscript," I sent a copy, among others, to the President of the Academy of Medicine, together with a note calling his attention to the matter. On the 28th of February I found the note, with pamphlet, on the table of the Chairman of the Surgical Section, to which it had been forwarded by the President for such action as it might think fit in the premises. Having been called upon to explain my views, I detailed the proposed plan of medical provision for railroads as contained in the said pamphlet, virtually the same as contained in the paper read before the State Medical Society, of which I also presented a copy. The plans were approved, and referred, on motion, to one of the members of the Section to express the sense of the meeting. A favorable report was made at a future meeting, but as I had not proposed any specific resolutions the subject dropped, and the sittings terminated for the season.

During the recess I wrote to the member above alluded to, stating that I should like to have the approval of the Surgical Section in such a form that I might be able to avail myself of it in advocating the measure, and proposed to read a supplementary paper and offer a set of resolutions. The Doctor promptly and kindly answered that he approved of my plan, and that it would be well to have my paper ready for the first meeting in October. Accordingly, at the meeting of the 28th of last month, as it was of importance that action should be taken previous to the meeting of the Legislature, Professor Flint yielded the floor for a sufficient time, the members assented, the foregoing paper was read, and the ACCOMPANYING RESOLUTIONS DULY SECONDED AND UNANIMOUSLY ADOPTED.

It was further proposed to send the paper to the regular meeting of the Academy of Medicine, so as to give it the endorsement of the entire body. It there still awaits action.

PROFESSIONAL AND OTHER ENDORSEMENTS.

In addition to the favorable action on the subject of medical provision for railroads by the two largest medical bodies of the State, and which will be found at the end of the respective papers, the following resolution was adopted :

WESTCHESTER CO. MEDICAL SOCIETY.

At the regular annual meeting of the Westchester County Medical Society, held at Yonkers, June 17th, 1862, the following resolution, offered by Dr. P. Stewart of Peekskill, was unanimously adopted, to wit:

Resolved, That we gladly take this opportunity to express our approval of the humanitary measure set forth in a paper entitled "On Medical Provision for Railroads as a Humanitarian Measure as well as a source of economy to the Companies," and read by the author at the last meeting of the New York State Medical Society, and that the President and Secretary of the Society are hereby ordered to sign their names officially to this resolution as an endorsement of such approval.

From the minutes.

T. SNOWDEN, M.D.,
Acting President for
J. FOSTER JENKINS, M.D.,
Absent on Sanitary Comm.

JAMES HART CURRY, Secretary.
YONKERS, *June* 17, 1862.

42

The following paper is signed by nearly all the Professors of Surgery in the New York Medical Schools:

"We cordially concur in the propriety and humanity of Dr. Arnold's plan of hospital stations along the line of railroads."

(Signed)

VALENTINE MOTT, M.D., LL.D., Emerit. Prof. of Surgery University of New York.

ALEX. H. STEVENS, M.D., LL.D., Emerit. Prof. of Clin. Surgery, Col. of Phys. and Surgeons.

JAMES ANDERSON, M.D., President of N. Y. Academy of Medicine.

H. D. BULKLEY, M.D., President N. Y. Co. Medical Society.

EDWD. DELAFIELD, M.D., President of Med. Depart. Columbia College.

WILLARD PARKER, M.D., Prof. of Surg. and Surg. Anat. Col. Phys. and Surgeons.

WM. H. VAN BUREN, M.D., Prof. of Anatomy Univ. of New York.

J. M. CARNOCHAN, M.D., Prof. Clin. and Operative Surg. N. Y. Med. Col.

JAMES R. WOOD, M.D., Prof. Opr. Surg. and Surg. Pathology, Bellevue Med. Col.

T. M. MARKOE, M.D., Adjunct Prof. of Surg. Col. Phys. and Surg.

ALFRED C. POST, M.D., Prof. of Surg. University of N.Y.

JOHN P. GARRISH, M.D., One of the Surgeons to Ophthalmic Hospital.

LEWIS A. SAYRE, M.D., Prof. Orthopœd. Surg. Bellevue Hosp. Med. Col.

[NOTE.—I have added the appointments of the respective signers for the benefit of distant and non-professional readers.   E. S. F. A.]

Extract of Letter from Dr. V. Mott.

1 GRAMERCY PARK, *February* 16, 1862.

DEAR DOCTOR,

* * * * You cannot fail, I think, in your humane undertaking, it is so good and self-evident.   * * *

Yours truly,

Dr. Arnold.   V. MOTT.

Extract of Letter from the Same.

FRIDAY, *February* 21, 1862.

DEAR DOCTOR,

* * * * Doubtless all Life Insurance Companies, when they are applied to, will, at a glance, see the importance of your noble project

It will not only strike them as humane, but it will appeal forcibly to their pockets, &c., &c.

Yours truly,

Dr. Arnold. V. Mott.

Letter from J. M. Carnochan, M.D., Prof. of Surgery and Surgeon-in-Chief at Ward's Island.

New York, February 15, 1862.

My Dear Sir,

I return you many thanks for your letter and valuable pamphlet "On Medical Provision for Railroads as a humanitarian measure as well as a source of Economy to Companies."

The project is one of vast utility, and, when perfected and matured as you already seem to have done, from its general applicability, will be adopted in all localities where civilization has advanced.

Communities as well as railroad companies owe you a debt of gratitude for bringing before the notice of the public your well-devised propositions, for, although perfectly simple when once stated, yet the practical form into which they have been arranged could only have been the result of much consideration and reflection.

With best regards to yourself and the sincere hope that your admirable project may soon be carried into effect, I remain, my dear sir,

Very truly yours,

To Dr. Edmund Arnold. J. M. Carnochan.

From Henry H. Smith, M.D., Late Surgeon-General of Pennsylvania, Prof. of Surgery University of Pennsylvania.

1112 Walnut street, Philadelphia, October 20, 1862.

Sir,

Your communication of October 1st, 1862, with the accompanying pamphlet "On Medical Provision for Railroads as a Humanitarian Measure," reached me two days since. You are entitled to the thanks of the community for originating so important and useful a measure, and I trust your efforts will be successful. If you will forward me a copy of the proposed bill I will take the necessary steps to obtain legislative action in Pennsylvania.

Very respectfully yours,

To Edmd. F. Arnold. Henry H. Smith.

From Alex. B. Mott, M.D., Prof. Surg. Anat. Bellevue Hospital Medical College, &c., &c.

New York, November 8, 1862.

My Dear Sir,

I have read with much interest your able and valuable pamphlet "On Medical Provision for Railroads as a Humanitarian Measure," &c., and trust that the important suggestions you have made, and the well-matured plans you have devised, will be adopted, feeling satisfied that many lives will thus be saved, and much suffering alleviated.

Wishing you success in your noble enterprise, believe me, my dear Doctor,

Yours very truly,

Edmd. S. F. Arnold, M.D., Yonkers.

ALEX. B. MOTT.

From Frank H. Hamilton, M.D., Prof. Military Surgery, Fractures, &c., Bellevue Hosp. Med. Col., &c. &c.,

ST. JOSEPH'S GENERAL HOSPITAL, U. S. A.
CENTRAL PARK, N. Y. *November 13th,* 1862.

DEAR SIR,

I listened to your paper, as read before the Surgical Section of the New York Academy of Medicine, and was delighted with the plan and scope of your project. It meets with my hearty approval. I trust you will succeed in carrying conviction to the minds of the State Legislators.

Very respectfully yours,

FRANK H. HAMILTON,
Surgeon in Charge.

Abstract of Letter from Dr. Peter Stewart of Peekskill.

January 16, 1862.

DR. ARNOLD—DEAR SIR,

* * * * I saw your article in the "Times," and read it carefully and approvingly. I did not know who the author was, of course, but I was forcibly struck with its suggestions. I am heartily glad you intend to present it before the State Medical Society. I shall (D. V.) be present at the meeting in February next, and if I can render you any service I shall be most happy to do so. I thank you for a copy of your pamphlet.

Very truly yours,

P. STEWART.

Abstract of Letter from Dr. G. J. Fisher of Sing Sing.

January 19th, 1862.

DR. ARNOLD, DEAR SIR,

* * * * I received and read, with much interest, your paper "On Medical Provision for Railroads." I highly approve of the proposed plan, and think you deserve the thanks of the profession and public for your humane consideration of the subject. I hope it will be put into practical operation soon. I have thought of the necessity of some ready means to relieve the wounded in cases of accident, and in view of the want of such means, I have for years past, when travelling by rail, taken with me my pocket case and some medicines, &c., &c.

Yours truly,

G. J. FISHER.

45

From A. H. Baker, M.D., Prof. of Surgery Cincinnati College of Medicine and Surgery.

CINCINNATI, *November* 18, 1862.

E. S. F. ARNOLD, M.D.—DEAR SIR,

I have examined the pamphlet on "Medical Provision for Railroads as a Humanitarian Measure as well as a source of Economy to Companies." The subject is one of vast importance, and the plan proposed should meet the approbation of all parties.

I hope, my dear sir, your labors may be rewarded by its adoption, and that you may long live to witness the beneficial results. With high consideration, I am,

Very truly yours,

A. H. BAKER.

From the American Medical Times, of January 25th, 1862.

In an editorial, written shortly after receiving my first small pamphlet on Medical Provision for Railroads and Steamboats, the following remarks are made:

"From carefully prepared statistics it appears that in this country, during 1861, there were 63 railroad accidents, resulting in 101 killed and 459 wounded; in 1860 there were 74 railroad accidents, resulting in 57 persons killed and 315 wounded. The number of railroad accidents for the last nine years was 1,040, giving 1,267 persons killed, and 4,385 wounded, &c. In reviewing such statistics the practical question which presents itself to every philanthropist is, how can modern travelling be rendered more safe? As physicians, it is not our province to discuss the causes of railroad and steamboat disasters. The case of the injured, however, falls to our lot, and we have a direct interest in whatever tends to make our services most available in the mitigation and relief of suffering." After recapitulating the leading features of my plan, the article goes on to say: "If this, or some similar plan, were adopted by our railroad authorities it cannot be doubted that many lives now lost would be saved, and much suffering would be promptly relieved after those terrible accidents, which so often thrill the community with terror."

In allusion to the paper on Medical Provision for Railroads as a Humanitarian Measure, &c., the same journal says:

"Dr. Arnold has been for a long time turning over in his mind the benefits that would result to the travelling public by the adoption of some reliable plan of action, and has finally brought the results of his investigations before the Society (N. Y. State Medical) in the form of an elaborate and well-timed paper. His suggestions are simple, efficient, and eminently practical, and they cannot fail to carry conviction to the mind of everyone interested in the preservation of life and limb on the national thoroughfares. The whole matter is now being brought up in the Legislature, where it is to be hoped that it will receive the grave consideration which it deserves."—*Ibid., February* 15, 1862.

From the Philadelphia Med. and Surg. Reporter of March 29, 1862.

"We have read with great pleasure the paper on this subject, placed by Dr. Edmund Arnold of Yonkers, N. Y., before the late meeting of the N. Y. State Medical Society. The paper is reprinted in pamphlet form, and undoubtedly widely circulated." [I may observe only privately until now.] The article, which is too long to be quoted entire, here, after recapitulating some of the leading facts and giving an outline of my plans, goes on to say: "Such are the essential features of the plan proposed by Dr. Arnold, and as a humanitarian measure it deserves serious consideration. If carried into operation upon all our railroads, the horrors of the 'accidents' frequently occurring would not only be greatly mitigated, but many valuable lives no doubt be saved, and our railroad companies would thus recognise a legal as well as moral obligation to guard against their occurrence. A double object would thereby be gained. Both the traveller and the company would be better protected, &c., &c." After inquiring whether my plan is not, however, more complicated than necessary, an objection which I have endeavored to answer in the second paper of this pamphlet, the article concludes as follows: "But these are only hints, intended to direct the profession more particularly to the subject, and we will only add, whatever may be the views in regard to the feasibility or practicability of the plan proposed by Dr. Arnold, his pamphlet is worthy of a careful perusal, and he is entitled to the gratitude of the whole community for discussing so important a subject with so much enthusiasm, humanity, and discretion."

From the New York Evening Post, January 13, 1862.

ON RAILROAD SURGEONS.—"It is somewhat remarkable, in this age of railway accidents, no one has before thought of the propriety of establishing a medical and surgical system in connection with our railroads, whereby speedy relief may be obtained for the victim of railway disaster. The life-boat and the fire-escape have materially lessened the chance of accident in other dangers which beset the traveller, but until now there has been no similar definite plan suggested as an accompaniment to our railway system. Our attention has been called to this by a little pamphlet 'On Medical Provision for Railroad Accidents,' a portion of which has previously been published as the communication of a Country Surgeon to the American Medical Times of Dec. 7, 1861. The writer, who has lived on the line of one of our great railroads and has witnessed some fearful accidents, proposes the establishment of a bureau of railway surgeons, in which he maintains that the public and railroad companies themselves, apart from higher considerations, are interested even as a matter of economy. His plan is as follows:" Here follows an outline of its general features, which I omit, after which the article continues: "Our space does not permit us to publish further extracts from the excellent and suggestive pamphlet, to which we refer all interested in the matter. The plan of the writer appears to be both humane and practical—humane, because it at once appeals to the sympathies, which everybody feels for the victim of sudden accident, and practical, because it will conduce as much to the benefit of railway companies as to that of travellers."

I shall conclude these extracts from journals with one from the Scottish American, in a review of my previously published pamphlet.

From the Scottish American Journal, February 20, 1862.

"The mere title-page of this little pamphlet by 'a Country Surgeon,' gives us an idea. Sidney Smith ventured to propose the immolation of a bishop or two to the Mumbo Jumbo who presides over these smashing disasters. *Punch*, we believe, has suggested that such accidents would not occur if a director were seated on the anterior and posterior buffers of each train. But we have never had anything *done* to prevent accidents, or rather nothing that has been done has prevented them. Are these railroad accidents, which at irregular intervals appal the public, fatalities? We fear that to some extent they are, and acknowledging that, the question arises, how can these evils be ameliorated? 'A Country Surgeon' (Dr. Arnold, of Yonkers, we believe,) answers this question in the pamphlet before us." Here follows a short outline of the main plan, after which the article concludes as follows: "Subsidiary to these main points the pamphlet gives many useful suggestions. It is a disinterested and well-considered effort for the public good, and we hope will meet with the attention from railway managers and railway travellers that it deserves."

I may add that all the arguments in the small pamphlet above referred to will be found in the present papers.